# What Happens at a
# Crayon Factory?

By Lisa M. Guidone

Reading Consultant: Susan Nations, M.Ed.,
author/literacy coach/consultant in literacy development

**WEEKLY READER®**
PUBLISHING

**Please visit our web site at www.garethstevens.com.**
**For a free catalog describing Gareth Stevens Publishing's list of high-quality books,**
**call 1-800-542-2595 (USA) or 1-800-387-3178 (Canada). Our fax: 877-542-2596**

**Library of Congress Cataloging-in-Publication Data**

Guidone, Lisa M.
    What happens at a crayon factory? / By Lisa M. Guidone.
        p. cm. — (Where people work)
    Includes bibliographical references and index.
    ISBN-10: 0-8368-9273-9   ISBN-13: 978-0-8368-9273-4 (lib. bdg.)
    ISBN-10: 0-8368-9372-7   ISBN-13: 978-0-8368-9372-4 (softcover)
    1. Crayons—Juvenile literature.   I. Title.
  TS1268.G85   2008
  688—dc22                             2008002973

This edition first published in 2009 by
**Weekly Reader® Books**
An Imprint of Gareth Stevens Publishing
1 Reader's Digest Road
Pleasantville, NY 10570-7000 USA

Senior Managing Editor: Lisa M. Herrington
Creative Director: Lisa Donovan
Designer: Alexandria Davis

Photo credits: All photos courtesy of Crayola. Crayola®, serpentines, and chevrons are trademarks
of Crayola. The publisher thanks Crayola for its participation in the development of this book.

Printed in the United States of America

2 3 4 5 6 7 8 9 10 09 08

Hi, Kids!

I'm Buddy, your Weekly Reader® pal. Have you ever visited a crayon factory? I'm here to show and tell what happens at a crayon factory. So, come on. Turn the page and read along.

**Boldface** words appear in the glossary.

What do you like to color? Have you ever wondered how crayons are made? Crayons are made in a **factory**.

Crayons are made from hot, melted **wax**. Colored powder called **pigment** is mixed into the wax. Pigment gives crayons their color.

**pigment**

A worker pours the colorful hot wax from a bucket into holes shaped like crayons. The holes are called **molds**.

molds

The crayon wax cools and gets hard. Look! Hard crayons pop out of the molds.

Crayons are put on a moving belt. The crayons travel to a machine. The machine puts paper **labels** on the crayons.

labels

Workers check the crayons. If they are not just right, they are put aside to be melted into another batch.

The good crayons then go to another machine. This machine sorts them by color.

17

The colorful crayons are placed into boxes. Then they are sent to stores.

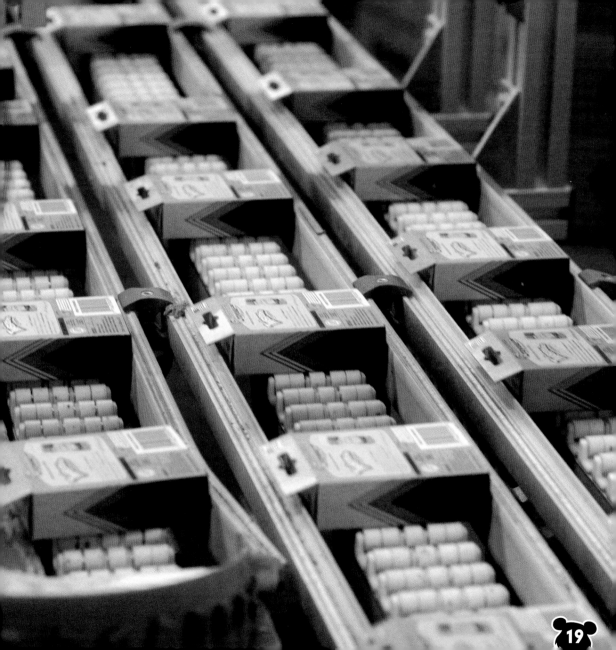

Red, green, yellow, and blue. The crayons are now ready for you!

# Glossary

**factory:** a place where machines and workers make things

**labels:** pieces of paper that are put on something to describe it

**molds:** open forms that keep hot liquid in a certain shape until it cools and becomes hard

**pigment:** a powder mixed with a liquid to give color

**wax:** a sticky substance used to make crayons

# For More Information

## Books

*From Wax to Crayon.* Robin Nelson
(Lerner Publications, 2003)

*Wax to Crayon.* Julie Murray (Buddy Books, 2006)

## Web Sites

**Crayola**

*www.crayola.com*

Find coloring pages, crafts, games, and more!

**PBS Kids: Mr. Rogers' House**

*www.pbskids.org/rogers/R_house/picpic.htm*

Visit this site for a great video, facts, and activity on how people make crayons.

**Publisher's note to educators and parents:** Our editors have carefully reviewed these web sites to ensure that they are suitable for children. Many web sites change frequently, however, and we cannot guarantee that a site's future contents will continue to meet our high standards of quality and educational value. Be advised that children should be closely supervised whenever they access the Internet.

 # Index

boxes  18

color  4, 6, 16

crayons  4, 6, 8, 10, 12, 14, 16, 18, 20

factory  4

labels  12

molds  8, 10

moving belt  12

pigment  6

powder  6

stores  18

wax  6, 8, 10

## About the Author

Lisa M. Guidone works in children's publishing. She has written and edited children's books and magazines for Weekly Reader for nearly eight years. She lives in Trumbull, Connecticut, with her husband, Ryan. She dedicates this book to her new nephew, Anthony, in hopes he shares her love of reading.